AUSTRALIA'S MOST EXTREME

By Kathy Riley

Australian GEOGRAPHIC

AUSTRALIA'S MOST EXTREME

Reprinted in 2019 by

54 Park Street, Sydney, NSW 2000
Telephone: (02) 9163 7214
Email: editorial@ausgeo.com.au

www.australiangeographic.com.au

Australian Geographic customer service:
1300 555 176 (local call rate within Australia).
From overseas +61 2 8667 5295

Printed in China by Leo Paper Products

Funds from the sale of this book go to support the Australian Geographic Society, a not-for-profit organisation dedicated to sponsoring conservation and scientific projects, as well as adventures and expeditions.

Editor Lauren Smith
Text Kathy Riley
Book design Mike Rossi
Creative director Mike Ellott
Picture research Jess Teideman
Sub-editor Carolyn Barry
Proof reader Ken Eastwood
Editor-in-Chief, Australian Geographic Chrissie Goldrick
Managing Director, Australian Geographic Jo Runciman

ALSO IN THIS SERIES:

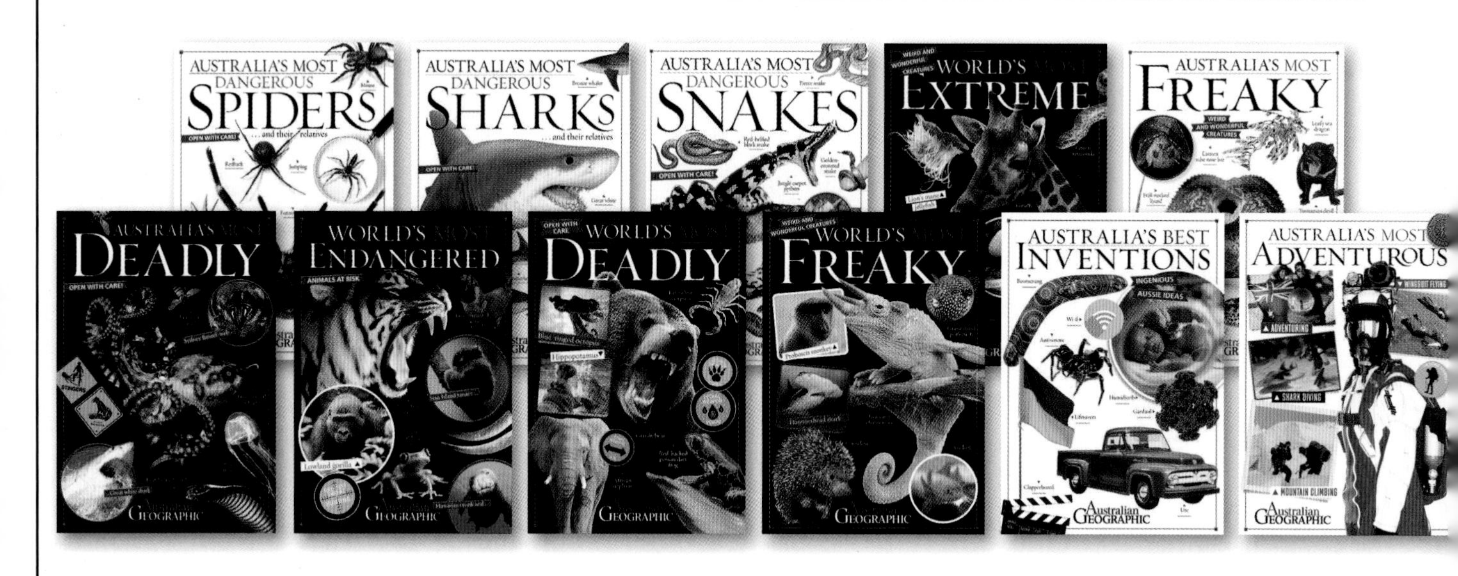

AUSTRALIA'S MOST
EXTREME

Life is tough in the animal kingdom, and survival depends on being the best at evading predators and finding food. These animals have developed some amazing abilities and characteristics in their quest to be the best. So turn the page and get ready to meet Australia's Most Extreme!

CONTENTS

EXTREMELY BIG!

Size Matters

Size can give a creature the edge it needs to survive in the animal world. A predator will think twice before attacking a larger animal, and being big can help when it comes to finding food and mates.

AUSTRALIA'S
LARGEST ANIMAL EVER!
MOST EXTREME

GREAT BARRIER REEF

The Great Barrier Reef, off the east coast of Australia, is the largest coral reef in the world. A coral reef is like an underwater city, built by tiny living animals called polyps. Many species of plant, fish and other organisms live together on a reef, just as lots of different animals and plants live in our cities.

EXTREME FACT!

The Great Barrier Reef stretches for more than 2300 kilometres!

EXTREME FACT!

A blue whale can grow up to 30 metres long and can eat up to 3600 kilograms of krill in one day!

◀ BLUE WHALE

The blue whale is the largest animal that has ever lived on Earth: it can weigh almost 200 tonnes – which is about as heavy as four train carriages. Its tongue alone is as heavy as an elephant! A blue whale gives birth to the world's largest newborn, with a weight of nearly three tonnes.

▶ WANDERING ALBATROSS

The wandering albatross has the longest wingspan of any bird – more than three metres, which is about the same as the width of a bus. Such long wings mean this bird can fly like a plane, gliding for hours without flapping its wings once.

◀ LION'S MANE JELLYFISH

The lion's mane jellyfish is the largest jellyfish in the world. The diameter of its body, or bell, can be about as long as a man; and its tentacles can grow to the length of a cricket pitch. Not only is it truly enormous, but it also glows in the dark!

EXTREMELY BIG!

▶ COCONUT CRAB

Can you picture a crab the size of a cat? The coconut crab can grow to 40 centimetres in length and weigh up to four kilograms! This **crustacean** gets its name from the coconuts it likes to eat, using its strong claws to strip away the outside of the coconut and then break it open.

True or False?

A coconut crab is strong enough to break your arm.

◀ SALTWATER CROCODILE

There is no bigger reptile in the world than the saltwater croc! Male salties can grow as long as seven metres, while females grow to about half that length. Their jaws are among the strongest of any animal in the world, capable of crushing a cow's skull.

▶ AUSTRALIAN PELICAN

We all love the Australian pelican, but did you know it has the world record for the largest bill of any bird? The male's bill is larger than the female's, and can grow to a length of 50 centimetres, or about as long as a man's arm.

EXTREME FACT!

A pelican's bill can hold 13 litres of water.

◀ DINGO

The dingo is the largest land-living predator in Australia. It has lived in Australia for thousands of years, and is one of the last truly wild dogs in the world. It's not much bigger than a kelpie, but the dingo is tough and very clever.

▶ SHIELD-BACKED KATYDID

At 13 centimetres long, the shield-backed katydid is one of the largest katydids in the world. It is found in Australia throughout rainforests on the Cape York Peninsula.

LITTLE LEGENDS

Being small does not necessarily mean being weak. In fact, sometimes being small is a great advantage. It's much easier to hide, for one thing!

▶ LITTLE FOREST BAT

AUSTRALIA'S SMALLEST BAT MOST EXTREME

One of Australia's smallest bats, weighing less than this page, the little forest bat has a wingspan of up to 15cm. It finds its way around by using **echolocation** - putting out special sound waves and using their echoes to create a picture of its surroundings.

True or False?

Bats are blind.

A: False

◀ SCANTY FROG

AUSTRALIA'S SMALLEST FROG MOST EXTREME

Even if you were lucky enough to hear the clicking call of the scanty frog, it would be almost impossible to find – it's less than two centimetres long, which is smaller than the size of your thumbnail. It is Australia's smallest frog species and it lives in rainforests in north Queensland.

◀ LITTLE PENGUIN

The little penguin is the smallest of the world's 17 types of penguin. A full-grown adult is about the same length as a ruler and weighs only a kilogram. Little penguins can be found living in **colonies** along the coast of southern Australia and Tasmania, as well as New Zealand.

Did you know?

In some fairy penguin colonies in Australia a type of dog called a maremma has been trained to protect the penguins from being eaten by foxes. That's a pretty special guard dog!

▶ STOUT INFANTFISH

This is the smallest Australian fish, and the second smallest fish in the world. It grows to a maximum length of eight millimetres, which is about the same length as your pinky fingernail. If you were to go to a seafood shop and ask for a kilo of stout infantfish, you'd be given one million of them!

EXTREMELY FAST!

SPEEDY SURVIVORS

Speed is a great tool for survival. Whether it's in the air, on the ground or in the sea, being super fast means an animal can zoom out of the way of attackers and chase down prey.

▶ PEREGRINE FALCON

The fastest animal in the world, the peregrine falcon coasts high above the ground until it spots something it wants to eat. Folding its wings flat against its body, the peregrine falcon drops into a dive, reaching speeds of more than 300 kilometres an hour. WHAM! Within seconds this powerful bird has plucked up its **prey** with its large, strong talons.

AUSTRALIA'S
1
FASTEST BIRD
MOST EXTREME

Did you know?

The peregrine falcon has a special pair of eyelids that helps protect its eyes and vision as it dives through the air.

▶ SAILFISH

AUSTRALIA'S
FASTEST FISH
MOST EXTREME

The record for the world's fastest fish goes to the sailfish. With a shape that's perfectly designed for moving fast through the water, the sailfish has been clocked going at 110 kilometres per hour. That's as fast as your mum or dad drives on the freeway!

TOP SPEED
110
km/h

TOP SPEED
70
km/h

◀ DRAGONFLY

AUSTRALIA'S
FASTEST FLYING INSECT
MOST EXTREME

The dragonfly is one of the fastest flying insects in the world, with larger species capable of speeds of up to 70 kilometres per hour. It's also incredibly nimble in the air: it can hover, fly in zigzags and go backwards.

▶ TIGER BEETLE

The fastest insect in Australia, this beetle reaches a top running speed of around nine kilometres per hour, which, for its size, is the same as a human running more than 700 kilometres per hour. It moves so fast that it goes blind while runnning because its brain can't process the visual images quickly enough.

TOP SPEED
9
km/h

AUSTRALIA'S
FASTEST LAND INSECT
MOST EXTREME

TRICKS AND TRAPS

AUSTRALIA'S SNEAKIEST LUNCH STEALER MOST EXTREME

Some animals can't be the biggest, the strongest or the fastest, so instead they have become the sneakiest! These animals use a range of very clever tricks to help them survive.

◀ CHRISTMAS ISLAND FRIGATEBIRD

Frigatebirds have a very sneaky way of getting their food: they steal it! They chase other seabirds until the chased birds **regurgitate** their meal. Then the frigatebird eats the vomited food! Male frigatebirds have enormous red throat pouches, and during the breeding season they puff them up like big red balloons to attract female birds.

▶ CHANNEL-BILLED CUCKOO

When the channel-billed cuckoo is ready to lay her egg, she chooses the nest of another bird! When laying her sneaky egg, she will often damage the other eggs in the nest. When the egg hatches, the young cuckoo is cared for by the mother of the original eggs.

BLUESTRIPED FANGBLENNY

The bluestriped fangblenny is a master of disguise: it can change colour to look like other fish. It does this for safety and for food. The fangblenny can change into many different colours, depending on which school of fish it wants to blend in with.

FACT BOX

Can't see me!

One of the best tricks in the animal kingdom is camouflage. Many creatures have patterns to help them blend in with their surroundings. Camouflage helps an animal hide from a predator, or allows them to sneak up on prey. Can you think of any animals that use camouflage?

▶ ANGLERFISH

Anglerfish dangle a glowing or wormlike bait, called an esca, from a long lure that sticks out from the front of its head like a fishing rod. It then waits until a hungry fish comes to investigate. Then WHAM! It gobbles down its prey with lightning speed.

EXTREME ENVIRONMENTS

EXTREME SURVIVORS

There are some places that are so extreme only a handful of animals can live there. These animals have developed some very special tools to help them meet the challenges of their environment.

TARDIGRADE

This animal is no bigger than a flea, but it is by far the toughest animal on Earth! It can survive temperatures hotter than 150°C and colder than –200°C. It can go nearly 10 years without water. It could go six times deeper than the deepest point in the ocean and still survive the pressure.

AUSTRALIA'S TOUGHEST SURVIVOR MOST EXTREME

EMPEROR PENGUIN

In the middle of winter, Antarctica is the coldest place on Earth, with temperatures plunging to below –60°C. Emperor penguins are some of the only wild animals to spend winter in such a place, and they also breed in this freezing weather!

AUSTRALIA'S COLDEST HOME MOST EXTREME

▲ DEEP-SEA HATCHETFISH

The hatchetfish uses special cells on its belly to put out a level of light that is exactly the same as the water it is swimming in. This means that it hides its own shadow from would-be predators lurking below. In other words, it makes itself invisible!

EXTREME FACT!

The tardigrade has been taken into space…and of course, it survived!

▶ WATER-HOLDING FROG

The water-holding frog has developed some amazing tricks to help it survive without water. During drought, it buries itself, and enters a kind of sleep, where its organs almost shut down, conserving water and energy. One type of water-holding frog can go as long as seven years underground without food or water!

EXTREMELY LONG!

GREAT LENGTHS

These animals have developed superhero ability when it comes to jumping, flying, diving and gliding!

AUSTRALIA'S LONGEST GLIDING MAMMAL MOST EXTREME

SUGAR GLIDER

The sugar glider is an adorable little animal that lives in trees in forests across Australia. It has a very clever way of travelling from tree to tree: instead of climbing, it glides. The sugar glider has a special furry **membrane**, like a cloak, which is attached to its wrists and ankles. When it wants to glide, it launches itself from a tree branch, spreads its arms and legs out wide and floats through the air using its big tail to steer.

EXTREME FACT!

The sugar glider can glide through the air for up to 100 metres – which is a VERY long way.

▶ RED KANGAROO

AUSTRALIA'S
LONGEST JUMPER
MOST EXTREME

A red kangaroo can hop 13 metres in one jump – as long as a bus! Kangaroos have very powerful hind legs that act like springs, and a big tail to help with balance. When it gets going, a kangaroo can jump along at great speed, while using relatively little energy.

Q&A

Q: What do you call a group of kangaroos?

A: A mob.

▼ CUVIER'S BEAKED WHALE

Scientists have recorded a Cuvier's beaked whale diving to a depth of nearly three kilometres and staying underwater for two hours and 17 minutes – which is the deepest and longest dive recorded for any mammal in the world.

AUSTRALIA'S
DEEPEST DIVING MAMMAL
MOST EXTREME

AUSTRALIA'S
MOST TRAVELLED BIRD
MOST EXTREME

▲ SHORT-TAILED SHEARWATER

This Australian seabird flies right around the globe every single year – that's a distance of up to 30,000 kilometres! During the breeding season, millions of these birds land along the coast of Australia to breed and lay eggs in burrows.

EXTREMELY EXTINCT

GIANTS OF THE PAST

Millions of years ago Australia was a very different place, where marsupial lions, giant kangaroos and wombats the size of cars roamed across the country.

▲ THUNDERBIRD

Taller than an emu and five times as heavy, this flightless bird would have sounded just like thunder thumping through the bush! It had big, powerful legs with enormous claws. It also had a big strong beak, which it used to eat fruit, nuts and maybe small animals.

EXTREME FACT!

The diprotodon would have been just a bit smaller than a hippopotamus!

◀ MARSUPIAL LION

A lion in Australia? Hard to believe, but it's true – thousands of years ago, Australia was home to a powerful predator about the size of a leopard, with fiercely sharp claws and teeth designed to slice through flesh and bone.

▶ GIANT KANGAROO

The giant short-faced kangaroo was about the same height as a red kangaroo but more than twice as heavy. Instead of a graceful snout, it had a thick, flat face, and long arms and fingers on its hands for pulling down branches to eat leaves.

True or False?

Kangaroos can swim.

A: True

◀ DIPROTODON

Can you picture a wombat the size of a car? With a length of about four metres and a weight of nearly three tonnes, the diprotodon had thick limbs, a big belly and strong front teeth for eating plants and shrubs. They lived throughout Australia, and they coexisted with Aboriginal people for a while before they became extinct.

What happened to our megafauna?

We know that these giants roamed around Australia for about two million years, and by 40,000 years ago they had all disappeared. But nobody knows exactly what killed them. Some scientists think they were hunted to extinction by indigenous Australians, or that a change in climate caused them to die out.

◀ TASMANIAN TIGER

The Tassie tiger was the world's largest known meat-eating **marsupial**. Although no one has seen a Tasmanian tiger for nearly 80 years, some people believe they still exist. If they do, they're very good at hiding!

Did you know?

The last known Tasmanian tiger died in a zoo in Hobart in 1936.

EXTREMELY SMART!

CLEVER CREATURES

They might not be able to do your maths homework, but these animals have shown they are extremely smart!

AUSTRALIA'S SMARTEST BUILDERS MOST EXTREME

TERMITES

Magnetic termites are found only in the Northern Territory. They build mounds that are very cleverly designed to help them survive all kinds of weather – hot, cold or even floods! The mounds are more than twice the size of a human, and they're built in flat shapes along an axis that helps them avoid the full force of the hot sun.

▶ MISTLETOE BIRD

It's true: the mistletoebird is the only bird that wipes its bottom on a branch after it has pooped! The mistletoebird only eats the berries of a plant called mistletoe. Mistletoe grows on the branches of other trees, so by wiping their poop (which contains seeds) on branches, the mistletoebirds are 'planting' mistletoe.

Q: What do you call a group of ravens?

A: An unkindness.

◀ RAVENS

Ravens are one of the most intelligent animals in the world! They belong to a family of birds called corvids, who have been recorded doing very intelligent things. They've been known to reel in fishermen's lines to eat their fish, use sticks as tools to get food, and even drop nuts onto roads so that cars will drive over the nuts and crack them so they can eat them!

◀ HUMPBACK WHALES

Forming a team of up to a dozen, these clever whales 'trap' schools of fish by creating a net of bubbles around them. The whales bring their bubble net in tighter, rising toward the surface, and then GULP! The whales lunge and take a mouthful of fish in one go!

EXTREMELY TOUGH!

TOUGH ENOUGH

Tough animals are ones that have special characteristics or abilities to help them survive difficult conditions. They don't have to be big – even a turtle or a beetle can be totally tough!

GREEN SEA TURTLE

AUSTRALIA'S 1 TOUGHEST DIET MOST EXTREME

The box jellyfish might be one of the deadliest animals in the world, but that doesn't make it safe from all predators! The **venom** of the box jellyfish doesn't hurt the green sea turtle, so the turtle can happily eat one of these killers for lunch. No matter how tough an animal is, there's always another one that is tougher!

FACT BOX Plastic bags kill turtles

Turtles like to eat jellyfish. Unfortunately, a turtle can easily mistake a plastic bag for a tasty jellyfish. When a turtle swallows a plastic bag it can get very sick and die. You can help keep turtles safe by not using too many plastic bags, and by keeping your rubbish out of the ocean.

BOMBARDIER BEETLE

AUSTRALIA'S 1 TOUGHEST SELF DEFENCE MOST EXTREME

This beetle carries the ingredients for a bomb in its bottom! When it is threatened, it mixes the chemicals together to create an explosion, making a large bang!

◀ TASMANIAN DEVIL

The Tasmanian devil might be small but it has a big bite – the same strength as a dog four times its size. This is mainly due to its diet: Tasmanian devils eat lots of meat, so they have to be able to crunch bones and tear through big chunks of flesh.

▶ LACE MONITOR

Lace monitors are built tough, with a strong body up to two metres long, a muscular tail and long, sharp claws. In spring, the males can get extremely aggressive, often getting into violent fights. They stand on their back legs and wrestle each other with their forelegs.

Did you know?

The bombardier beetle can produce as many as 80 explosions in four minutes!

EXTREME FACTS!

EXTRA EXTREME

Here are some more amazing animal facts and feats!

◀ ARCHER FISH

The archer fish has a pretty extreme way of getting its meal: it spits out a jet of water that knocks an insect off a leaf and into the water so it can snap it up! Archer fish are extremely accurate and able to hit an insect up to three metres away.

▶ QUOKKA

There's not much you can find that's not cute about the quokka! Quokkas can be found in south-western Western Australia – in particular, on Rottnest Island, where their relaxed and friendly nature has won over the hearts of many visiting tourists.

◀ GIANT BURROWING COCKROACH

This is the world's heaviest cockroach species, weighing up to 30 grams, which is about as heavy as two 50 cent coins. This **arthropod** can be as big as the palm of your hand!

◀ KOALA

A koala will sleep as much as 20 hours each day. The reason they need so much sleep is because the gum leaves they eat are difficult to digest and low in nutrients, so the koala sleeps to save energy.

True or False?

Koalas don't need to drink water.

A: True. They get the water they need from gum leaves; however, they can drink if necessary.

▲ MAGNIFICENT RIFLEBIRD

The male magnificent riflebird goes to very showy lengths to impress a female, plunging into a wonderful dance routine. Fanning his wings, he throws back his head, and hops up and down, flicking his wings and swinging his head from side to side.

EXTREMELY NOISY!

LOUD AND PROUD

Cover your ears! These animals use sound to stand out from the crowd, find mates and communicate.

DOUBLE DRUMMER

Cicadas are the loudest of all the insects, and the double drummer is up there with the noisiest. Once it gets going, it can produce a song that's louder than a jackhammer! Cicadas make their sound in their **abdomen**, by vibrating a membrane extremely quickly.

AUSTRALIA'S MOST EXTREME
LOUDEST INSECT

True or False?

Only the male cicada sings.

A: True

FACT BOX

Bird Chatter

There are lots of bird species that are able to copy, or mimic, the sounds of other birds, people and things around them. The lyrebird is Australia's most famous mimic, capable of copying the calls of up to 20 other birds, as well as things like chainsaws and cameras.

AUSTRALIA'S MOST EXTREME
BEST COPYCAT

BARKING OWL

This owl, which is quite common throughout Australia, has two different calls: one sounds like a dog barking; the other, a wailing woman. When early Australian settlers first heard the sound, they thought it was a woman screaming for help, and they would rush to try and find her!

In 2013, a golden retriever named Charlie from Adelaide broke the Guinness World Record for the loudest bark in the world. Six-year-old Charlie registered a bark that was 113.1 **decibels**. Even though his bark can be louder than a live rock band, Charlie's owner says he's usually a very quiet dog!

BIZARRE BEASTS

Some animals are so strange it's hard to believe they are real. It just goes to show how amazing the animal kingdom can be!

BLUE SEA SLUG

AUSTRALIA'S WEIRDEST SEA SLUG MOST EXTREME

This vibrant blue sea slug grows to about four centimetres long, about the length of your thumb. It feasts on bluebottles, whose stingers often entangle swimmers. It stores the bluebottle's stings in the tips of its feathery 'fingers' and uses them for its own protection.

Did you know?

The blue sea slug actually floats on its back. It fills up a sac in its stomach with gas to help it float.

GASTRIC BROODING FROG

AUSTRALIA'S WEIRDEST PARENTING MOST EXTREME

The female gastric brooding frog swallows her eggs, and they hatch inside her stomach, then they come out through her mouth! This frog became extinct in the 1980s, but in 2013, scientists took the first step towards bringing this frog back by creating a live **embryo**!

▶ TREE KANGAROO

This is one strange kangaroo! It lives in trees, eating leaves and fruit. It has muscled forearms (for climbing trees) and short hind legs, and a small snout. In fact, it looks more like a small bear with a long tail!

AUSTRALIA'S MOST EXTREME
WEIRDEST KANGAROO

EXTREME FACT!

A giant tree-kangaroo lived in Australia thousands of years ago. It was the size of a red kangaroo!

◀ ASSASSIN SPIDER

The assassin spider is a highly unusual type of spider, in that it has a neck – which is often very long – and long jaws that it uses to spear other spiders. Assassin spiders stalk and then stab their spider prey with their jaws, which are tipped with venomous fangs.

AUSTRALIA'S MOST EXTREME
WEIRDEST SPIDER

EXTREMELY COLOURFUL!

RAZZLE DAZZLERS

AUSTRALIA'S BRIGHTEST SLUG MOST EXTREME

Bright animals aren't just showing off – they use their colours to attract mates or prey, or to warn that they are dangerous!

◀ MOUNT KAPUTAR SLUG

These bright pink slugs are about 20 centimetres long, which is about the same as the distance from your wrist to your elbow. They hide during the day, and at night they climb trees to feast on moss and algae growing on tree trunks.

▶ MANTIS SHRIMP

While this shrimp looks pretty, it is one fierce crustacean. It has a pair of club-shaped limbs that it uses to deliver the fastest punch of any animal. The force of the punch is so great that it is capable of breaking the glass wall of an aquarium!

AUSTRALIA'S BRIGHTEST SHRIMP MOST EXTREME

▶ LEICHHARDT'S GRASSHOPPER

This grasshopper is an incredibly rare Australian grasshopper, long thought to be extinct until it was rediscovered in 1971. It lives in Australia's Top End, where it feeds on a special selection of plants.

Q&A

Q: How many types of jewel beetle are there in Australia?

A: 1200

▼ JEWEL BEETLE

Australia is a treasure trove when it comes to jewel beetles - we've got red, blue, spotted and - even **iridescent** ones! The key to their beauty lies in their outer skeleton, which reflects light in such a way as to create an unusually vibrant, shimmering colour.

Did you know?

Scientists are trying to unlock the secrets of the jewel beetle, in order to try to develop new types of paint.

Glossary

abdomen	**In an insect, the abdomen is the back part of the body.**
arthropod	**An animal from the group of non-vertebrates, including insects, spiders and crustaceans.**
colonies	**Groups of the same kind of animals living together.**
crustacean	**An arthropod with a hard outer shell that usually lives part of its life in the water, for example a lobster or a crab.**
decibel	**A unit of measurement for sound.**
echolocation	**A method of locating objects by making a noise and interpreting the echo which comes back.**
embryo	**An animal in the very early stages of its life.**
iridescent	**Having a sheen that reflects different colours.**
marsupial	**An animal with a pouch for developing babies.**
membrane	**A thin connecting layer.**
predator	**An animal that hunts and eats other animals.**
prey	**An animal that is hunted by other animals.**
regurgitate	**To bring back food that has been swallowed.**
venom	**A poison an animal produces and injects into another animal.**

Natural History Museum Book of Animal Records
Mark Carwardine, 2013, Firefly Books

101 Animal Records
Melvin Berger, 2013, Scholastic US

Amazing Animals Q&A
David Burnie, 2007, DK Publishing

The Animal Book: A Collection of the Fastest, Fiercest, Toughest, Cleverest, Shyest – and Most Surprising – Animals on Earth
Steve Jenkins, 2013, HMH Books for Young Readers

PHOTOGRAPHER AND ILLUSTRATOR CREDITS
Page numbers are followed by image position indicated clockwise from top left of page.

Alexandra Photos/Getty 11 (3); Allen, Mark/Australian Museum 9 (1); Auscape/Getty 26 (3), 28 (2); Barcroft Media/Getty Cover (2), 4 (2); Beckers, Dough/Flickr 8 (2); Belcher, Stephen/Minden Pictures/Getty 6 (1); Benjamint444/Wikimedia 31 (1); Bridger, Mark/Getty 16 (1); Brightling, Geoff/Getty 23 (3); Dingle, Craig/Getty 26 (2); Jason Edwards/NGS/Getty 15 (1); Eye of Science/Getty Front Cover (1), 3 (1), 14 (1); Fallows, Chris and Monique/Nature PL 11 (1); Field Museum Library/Getty Back cover (1); Fleetham, David/Visuals Unlimited/Science Photo Library 22 (1); Furlan, Borut/Getty 12 (1), 32 (1); Gibbons, Bob/SPL/Getty Back Cover (7); Gouldhurst, Nicholas/Getty Front cover (7); Gregory, Andrew/Australian Geographic 24 (2); Guiotto, Ego/Australian Geographic 23 (2); Hatcher, Bill/Australian Geographic 29 (1); Henderson, Alan/Minibeast Wildlife 11 (2); Holden, Heath/Getty Front Cover (3); Hoskin, Conrad 8 (3); Kaehler, Wolfgang/Getty 5 (1); Kushner, Brian E./Getty 3 (2), 10 (1); McDonald, Joe/Getty 16 (2); Minden Pictures/Getty Front Cover (6); Mint Images/Frans Lanting/Getty 14 (2); Mora, Roman Garcia/Stocktrek Images/Getty Back Cover (5); Murphy, Michael/NPWS 30 (3); Naoi, Ippei/Getty 4 (1); Nieminski, Craig 31 (1); Riviere, Patrick/Getty 9 (2); Rohrlach, Sylke/Flickr 28 (1); Schafer, Kevin/ Getty 20 (2); Semenov, Alexander/Getty 5 (2); Shakespeare, Russell/Australian Geographic 1 (1), 26 (1); Shutterstock Front Cover (4-5), Back Cover (2-4), 6 (2), 7 (2-3), 8 (1), 13 (1), 15 (3), 18 (1), 20 (3-4), 23 (1), 24 (3), 25 (1), 27 (1), 30 (2), 31 (2), Ends; Spence, Murray/Australian Geographic 7 (1); Stocker, Les/Getty Back Cover (6); Surman, Chris/Christmas Island Tourism Association 12 (3); Taylor, Kim/Warren Photographic 24 (1); Tier Und Naturfotografie J und C Sohns/Getty 17 (1); Todd Pusser/SeaPics.com 17 (3); Trusler, Peter/Australia Post 18 (2-4), 19 (1-2); Wegener, Jan/BIA/Getty 20 (1), 21 (1); Wikimedia Commons 12 (2), 17 (2), 29 (2); Willis, Martin/ Minden Pictures/Getty 25 (2); Zankel, Solvin/Visuals Unlimited/Science Photo Library 15 (2)